ALA Survey of Librarian Salaries 2002

Mary Jo Lynch, *Project Director*

ALA Survey Report

American Library Association
Office for Research and Statistics

American Library Association
Chicago 2002

ISBN 0-8389-8206-9

ISSN 0747-7201

Copyright © 2002 by the American Library Association.
All rights reserved except those which may be granted by Sections 107
and 108 of the Copyright Revision Act of 1976.

Printed in the United States of America.

Acknowledgments

Thanks are due to the many respondents who completed our questionnaires. Without their cooperation, this report would not be possible. We are grateful to the Association of Research Libraries (ARL) for sharing data with us as described in Appendix C and especially to Martha Kyrillidou, ARL Senior Program Officer for Statistics and Measurement, who sent the data electronically. We are also grateful to Ed Lakner, Diane LaBarbera, Lidan Luo, Anita Michel, Amie Whittemore and other staff at the Library Research Center of the Graduate School of Library and Information Science at the University of Illinois who managed the mailings and processed the returns. Appendix A was prepared by Maxine Moore, Program Officer in ALA's Office for Human Resource Development and Recruitment. Finally, thanks are due to Kathy Bork, Administrative Assistant in the Office for Research and Statistics (ORS) for word processing the revised text and tables.

Table of Contents

Acknowledgements   iii

Introduction   1

Results   3

Director/Dean   4
Deputy/Associate/Assistant Directors   7
Department Heads/Coordinators/Senior Managers   10
Managers/Supervisors of Support Staff   13
Librarians who do not supervise   16
Beginning Librarians   19

Discussion

Summary of Results   22
     Salaries by Type of Position   22
     Salaries by Type of Library   22
     Salaries by Region of the U.S.   23
     Problem with Categories New in 1999   23

Complicating Factors   23
     Meaning of "Full-Time"   23
     Meaning of "Professional"   23
     Salaries Below $22,000   23
     Job Levels or Faculty Ranks   24
     Level of Experience   24

Appendixes

A. Compensation Surveys Providing Information on Library Workers   25
B. ALA Policies Relating to Compensation Issues   32
C. Technical Considerations   36
D. Cover Letter   41
E. Survey Questionnaire   42
F. Salaries Paid for Less than a 12-month Year in Academic Libraries   47

Introduction

Librarians, the people who hire them, and interested others often ask the American Library Association (ALA) to tell them what salary might be paid to a librarian in a particular type of position, working in a particular type of library, in a particular part of the U.S. To fill the need for information of this kind, ALA began conducting a periodic survey of salaries for full-time professionals in academic and public libraries. Reports were published biennially from 1982 to 1988 and became annual in 1989.

This report, the eighteenth in a series, is similar to its predecessors in many ways but different in one important way which is described at the end of this Introduction. Otherwise, the 2002 report shares the following characteristics with its predecessors:

- It is based on salaries paid as of April 1st of the survey year.

- It is based on a survey of **libraries**, not individual librarians.

- It is based on a survey of **full-time** positions.

- It is based on a survey of **public and academic** libraries only. (Sources for salaries in other libraries are given in Appendix A.)

- It is based on a survey of libraries with at least **two professionals**. (See Appendix C for how this term is defined for public libraries and for academic libraries.)

- The public and academic library universe is stratified by the same **type/size criteria**: public libraries serving populations of from 25,000 to 99,999, public libraries serving populations of 100,000 or more, two-year colleges, four-year colleges, and universities. (The last category includes all institutions offering work beyond the bachelor's level).

- The nation is stratified into the same **geographic areas**: North Atlantic, Great Lakes and Plains, Southeast, West and Southwest (see Appendix C for list of states).

- It shows the **first quartile, median, and third quartile** for salaries paid in each type/size of library and region in addition to the **mean and range** (low and high) for each position reported.

- It shows salaries paid to staff **with master's degrees from programs in library and information studies accredited by ALA.**

- It shows salaries for **beginning librarians** in both public and academic libraries.

In the 1999 report, there was a change in how positions were described. Since the beginning, the ALA survey has collected salary data on staff holding three administrative positions (director, deputy/associate/assistant director, department/branch head) and three positions described in terms of content of work (reference/information librarian, cataloger/classifier, children's/young adult librarian). For 1999, the top two administrative positions remained and all other positions were collapsed into three, which focus on the nature of responsibility for the work of other staff: Department Heads/Coordinators/Senior Managers, Managers/Supervisors of Support Staff, and Librarians who do not supervise. This 2002 report used those same categories.

The changes were made for the following reasons:

1. The personnel systems in many libraries are not set up to provide the kind of information we were requesting (i.e., by position title related to job content).

2. Recent technological developments have led to the creation of many new positions in libraries. Although the titles are not standardized enough to warrant use in a survey instrument, without the salaries paid to staff in those positions, the results would not adequately represent the reality of the job market.

The Library Research Center of the University of Illinois Graduate School of Library and Information Science performed the mailing, processing, and computer analysis of the questionnaires. Mary Jo Lynch, Director of ALA's Office for Research and Statistics (ORS), directed the project and wrote this report.

Note: Since 1994, this annual salary survey has included unique "Supplementary Questions" which gathered information on an issue related to library personnel. For 2002, the questions were as follows:

Because of recent publicity about the shortage of librarians, ALA is often asked questions such as: How many positions are vacant at any one point in time? Do vacancies exist equally in all regions? What are the main reasons why positions are hard to fill? Your answers to the following questions will help us respond to those inquiries.

1. As of April 1, 2002, are there any full-time MLS positions for which funding is available that are vacant in your library? (Circle the appropriate number)

    Yes (Please continue) 1
    No (Please skip Question 5)............. 2

2. How many full-time MLS positions are now vacant? Report only funded positions.

    _____ vacant positions

3. Of the number reported above, how many have been vacant for six months or more?

    _____ positions vacant six months or more

4. Please consider the following list of reasons why the position(s) reported in Questions 4 is (are) still vacant, select up to three as the most likely. (Circle the appropriate numbers)

    Low salaries at your institution 1
    High cost of living in the area 2
    Geographic location of library... 3
    Lack of MLS degree holders generally... 4
    Shortage of people with particular specialty (e.g., children, science,
        technical services)... 5
    Lack of technical expertise 6
    Lack of management expertise.. 7
    Other (please specify)... 8

Have the events of September 11th caused a reduction in the numbers of funded positions vacant in your library? (Circle the appropriate number)

    Yes.. 1
    No.. 2

Results will be published in late 2002 in *Library Personnel News* and will be posted on the ORS website (http://www.ala.org/hrdr/employment.html).

Results

The survey questionnaire was mailed to 1,320 randomly selected libraries on April 11, 2002. Samples were drawn from twenty groups of libraries formed by stratifying five type-of-library categories by four regions of the U. S. Appendix D describes how groups were formed and sampled. By the end of June, usable responses had been received from 924 libraries, 70.0 percent of those sampled.

The results of this survey are presented on the following pages in six sets of tables. There are three pages of tables for each position. The first table presents salaries paid in medium-sized public libraries, i.e., those serving between 25,000 and 99,999. For each of four regions of the country and for the nation as a whole, the table shows the number of positions reported (N), the lowest salary and the highest salary (range), the mean (arithmetic average), the first quartile, median, and third quartile. This pattern is repeated for large public libraries (i.e., those serving populations of 100,000 or more), and for libraries in two-year colleges, four-year colleges, and in universities (i.e., institutions offering work beyond the baccalaureate degree).

The following example illustrates how to interpret the tables. In the first table for the position of director--the table presenting salaries paid in medium-sized public libraries--there were 86 salaries reported from the North Atlantic region. The lowest of these was $33,000 and the highest was $130,564. When all the salaries were added together and the result was divided by the total number (86) the average or mean was $71,148. When all the salaries were arrayed from low to high, 25 percent of them fell below $59,000, the first quartile, 50 percent fell below $67,533, the median, and 50 percent were above $67,533. Seventy-five percent fell below $82,700, the third quartile, and 25 percent were above that amount. The middle 50 percent of the salaries fell between $59,000 and $82,700.

Two caveats should be observed in reading the tables. The higher the number of cases (N), the more reliable the results of the sample in giving a true picture of the total population. When the number of cases is less than twenty-five, the results should be used with caution. This caution is especially applicable to the regional data for libraries where the number of professional staff is often small--medium sized public libraries, four-year colleges, and two-year colleges. Another caveat is that when the mean and the median are not close together, the mean is being influenced by some unusual values. When the mean is much higher than the median, there are several very high salaries. When the mean is much lower than the median, there are several very low salaries

DIRECTOR/DEAN

(Page 1 of 3)

Chief officer of the library or library system

Medium-sized Public Library
(Serving a population of from 25,000 to 99,999)

	Mean	First Quartile	Median	Third Quartile
North Atlantic N = 86 Range = $33,000 - $130,564	71,148	59,000	67,533	82,700
Great Lakes & Plains N = 84 Range = $39,027 - $121,000	70,184	56,556	70,510	79,858
Southeast N = 46 Range = $32,664 - $83,512	55,734	49,152	54,214	61,200
West & Southwest N = 55 Range = $40,049 - $136,000	72,095	57,000	67,864	87,816
All Regions N = 271 Range = $32,664 - $136,000	68,425	55,000	65,000	78,750

Large Public Library
(Serving a population of 100,000 or more)

	Mean	First Quartile	Median	Third Quartile
North Atlantic N = 36 Range = $56,606 - $200,000	89,990	69,791	84,655	105,868
Great Lakes & Plains N = 46 Range = $54,306 - $140,000	92,392	76,237	87,120	105,655
Southeast N = 50 Range = $37,500 - $138,582	84,167	64,805	79,580	101,852
West & Southwest N = 60 Range = $62,169 - $176,832	104,898	85,601	105,497	118,968
All Regions N = 192 Range = $37,500 - $200,000	93,708	75,000	91,255	109,039

Source: ALA Survey of Librarian Salaries, 2002

Director/Dean (Page 2 of 3)

Chief officer of the library or library system

Two-Year College

	Mean	First Quartile	Median	Third Quartile
North Atlantic N = 26 Range = $29,030 - $96,299	61,293	50,882	62,176	69,424
Great Lakes & Plains N = 22 Range = $34,500 - $92,000	59,320	45,291	59,850	69,749
Southeast N = 34 Range = $37,800 - $76,000	56,762	49,600	57,213	60,304
West & Southwest N = 28 Range = $42,144 - $107,000	62,415	52,360	59,000	70,912
All Regions N = 110 Range = $29,030 - $107,000	59,783	50,775	58,169	68,100

Four-Year College

	Mean	First Quartile	Median	Third Quartile
North Atlantic N = 32 Range = $32,960 - $118,500	67,097	49,110	58,221	87,557
Great Lakes & Plains N = 30 Range = $29,500 - $80,738	55,181	45,787	55,037	62,153
Southeast N = 29 Range = $31,000 - $70,890	47,088	35,138	46,350	58,250
West & Southwest N = 13 Range = $37,750 - $72,723	54,219	45,475	50,000	65,235
All Regions N = 104 Range = $29,500 - $118,500	56,471	43,537	53,100	63,545

Source: ALA Survey of Librarian Salaries, 2002

Director/Dean (Page 3 of 3)

Chief officer of the library or library system

University

	Mean	First Quartile	Median	Third Quartile
North Atlantic N = 49 Range = $40,038 - $196,600	92,583	66,450	85,000	105,500
Great Lakes & Plains N = 53 Range = $36,000 - $146,424	80,150	54,428	81,000	102,262
Southeast N = 57 Range = $41,310 - $160,000	82,303	62,572	76,683	96,599
West & Southwest N = 50 Range = $45,000 - $162,000	92,450	71,005	84,855	113,199
All Regions N = 209 Range = $36,000 - $196,600	86,594	63,188	81,032	102,762

All Academic and Public Libraries

	Mean	First Quartile	Median	Third Quartile
North Atlantic N = 229 Range = $29,030 - $200,000	77,011	58,898	72,496	90,500
Great Lakes & Plains N = 235 Range = $29,500 - $146,424	73,847	55,855	72,312	87,497
Southeast N = 216 Range = $31,000 - $160,000	68,328	52,527	61,509	79,044
West & Southwest N = 206 Range = $37,750 - $176,832	84,146	60,324	79,065	104,043
All Regions N = 886 Range = $29,030 - $200,000	75,714	56,595	71,444	91,023

Source: ALA Survey of Librarian Salaries, 2002

DEPUTY/ASSOCIATE/ASSISTANT DIRECTORS

Persons who report to the Director and manage major aspects of the library operation. (e.g., technical services, public services, collection development, systems/automation)

Medium-sized Public Library
(Serving a population of from 25,000 to 99,999)

	Mean	First Quartile	Median	Third Quartile
North Atlantic N = 65 Range = $27,403 - $106,169	56,980	46,500	56,000	66,148
Great Lakes & Plains N = 99 Range = $27,851 - $83,068	49,361	40,433	46,700	54,794
Southeast N = 46 Range = $26,316 - $62,000	42,789	36,061	42,876	48,150
West & Southwest N = 42 Range = $26,592 - $108,000	55,200	39,958	53,324	70,833
All Regions N = 252 Range = $26,316 - $108,000	51,100	40,367	48,047	58,642

Large Public Library
(Serving a population of 100,000 or more)

	Mean	First Quartile	Median	Third Quartile
North Atlantic N = 107 Range = $25,160 - $152,880	74,712	52,915	68,503	88,068
Great Lakes & Plains N = 98 Range = $42,640 - $122,985	71,666	57,081	68,532	82,367
Southeast N = 136 Range = $31,968 - $119,088	61,794	44,854	59,966	77,104
West & Southwest N = 153 Range = $39,231 - $111,912	75,319	62,600	75,816	87,932
All Regions N = 494 Range = $25,160 - $152,880	70,739	56,063	69,067	84,265

Source: ALA Survey of Librarian Salaries, 2002

Deputy/Associate/Assistant Directors (Page 2 of 3)

Persons who report to the Director and manage major aspects of the library operation. (e.g., technical services, public services, collection development, systems/automation)

Two-Year College

	Mean	First Quartile	Median	Third Quartile
North Atlantic N = 2 Range = $47,000 - $63,559	55,280		55,280	
Great Lakes & Plains N = 6 Range = $23,040 - $120,659	53,414	32,010	41,892	73,665
Southeast N = 21 Range = $31,500 - $54,000	40,516	35,280	39,326	46,297
West & Southwest N = 23 Range = $37,272 - $95,055	57,244	43,200	53,500	71,373
All Regions N = 52 Range = $23,040 - $120,659	49,971	37,408	45,547	54,450

Four-Year College

	Mean	First Quartile	Median	Third Quartile
North Atlantic N = 31 Range = $25,000 - $68,190	48,554	40,384	50,821	57,000
Great Lakes & Plains N = 14 Range = $24,888 - $59,210	38,892	28,525	36,571	49,167
Southeast N = 18 Range = $26,460 - $52,000	34,549	29,401	30,750	41,250
West & Southwest N = 10 Range = $27,568 - $48,471	40,568	36,962	42,761	44,345
All Regions N = 73 Range = $24,888 - $68,190	42,154	32,240	41,000	51,411

Source: ALA Survey of Librarian Salaries, 2002

Deputy/Associate/Assistant Directors (Page 3 of 3)

Persons who report to the Director and manage major aspects of the library operation. (e.g., technical services, public services, collection development, systems/automation)

University

	Mean	First Quartile	Median	Third Quartile
North Atlantic N = 78 Range = $29,758 - $110,954	71,471	58,727	72,471	85,503
Great Lakes & Plains N = 69 Range = $27,000 - $98,917	65,156	55,276	66,459	77,193
Southeast N = 100 Range = $24,000 - $97,979	60,733	48,783	59,265	73,961
West & Southwest N = 114 Range = $28,000 - $109,776	68,291	53,469	64,747	82,854
All Regions N = 361 Range = $24,000 - $110,954	66,285	53,150	65,004	78,578

All Academic and Public Libraries

	Mean	First Quartile	Median	Third Quartile
North Atlantic N = 283 Range = $25,000 - $152,880	66,743	49,500	63,559	79,365
Great Lakes & Plains N = 286 Range = $23,040 - $122,985	60,387	45,924	58,006	73,597
Southeast N = 321 Range = $24,000 - $119,088	55,820	40,494	52,500	69,395
West & Southwest N = 342 Range = $26,592 - $111,912	68,274	53,381	67,442	83,544
All Regions N = 1,232 Range = $23,040 - $152,880	62,847	47,000	60,280	76,152

Source: ALA Survey of Librarian Salaries, 2002

DEPARTMENT HEADS/COORDINATORS/SENIOR MANAGERS
(Page 1 of 3)

Persons who supervise one or more professional librarians.

Medium-sized Public Library
(Serving a population of from 25,000 to 99,999)

	Mean	First Quartile	Median	Third Quartile
North Atlantic N = 165 Range = $30,084 - $82,159	48,263	40,556	45,511	54,218
Great Lakes & Plains N = 145 Range = $28,745 - $83,068	49,114	41,255	50,206	55,871
Southeast N = 22 Range = $22,500 - $69,917	41,952	32,665	41,822	53,131
West & Southwest N = 68 Range = $21,765 - $84,812	50,665	43,607	50,208	56,508
All Regions N = 400 Range = $21,765 - $84,812	48,633	41,000	48,298	55,451

Large Public Library
(Serving a population of 100,000 or more)

	Mean	First Quartile	Median	Third Quartile
North Atlantic N = 645 Range = $33,480 - $106,081	54,954	47,110	52,723	60,135
Great Lakes & Plains N = 600 Range = $31,811 - $84,840	54,496	46,680	52,750	61,499
Southeast N = 608 Range = $26,286 - $86,528	51,957	42,605	51,800	60,281
West & Southwest N = 831 Range = $31,524 - $95,700	58,703	50,832	57,895	66,914
All Regions N = 2,684 Range = $26,286 - $106,081	55,334	46,859	54,387	62,256

Source: ALA Survey of Librarian Salaries, 2002

Department Heads/Coordinators/Senior Managers (Page 2 of 3)

Persons who supervise one or more professional librarians.

Two-Year College

	Mean	First Quartile	Median	Third Quartile
North Atlantic N = 11 Range = $43,022 - $77,629	58,646	51,333	52,858	69,754
Great Lakes & Plains N = 9 Range = $38,700 - $97,800	68,294	43,850	77,333	91,999
Southeast N = 12 Range = $41,000 - $65,920	56,268	49,718	55,734	64,643
West & Southwest N = 15 Range = $30,098 - $58,999	46,958	42,198	45,250	53,318
All Regions N = 47 Range = $30,098 - $97,800	56,156	44,930	52,000	64,857

Four-Year College

	Mean	First Quartile	Median	Third Quartile
North Atlantic N = 17 Range = $29,615 - $62,618	46,288	35,000	46,560	56,910
Great Lakes & Plains N = 8 Range = $31,836 - $56,201	39,727	32,234	35,750	47,509
Southeast N = 12 Range = $25,000 - $55,130	37,013	31,250	35,969	40,646
West & Southwest N = 6 Range = $41,700 - $48,776	44,794	42,482	44,687	46,821
All Regions N = 43 Range = $25,000 - $62,618	42,271	35,000	41,194	49,260

Source: ALA Survey of Librarian Salaries, 2002

Department Heads/Coordinators/Senior Managers (Page 3 of 3)

Persons who supervise one or more professional librarians.

University

	Mean	First Quartile	Median	Third Quartile
North Atlantic N = 76 Range = $31,000 - $114,919	57,951	48,003	57,209	64,953
Great Lakes & Plains N = 86 Range = $32,000 - $87,341	52,580	44,445	50,988	60,218
Southeast N = 80 Range = $32,000 - $68,699	49,069	43,031	48,039	54,177
West & Southwest N = 73 Range = $33,000 - $89,436	55,276	43,001	50,160	66,479
All Regions N = 315 Range = $31,000 - $114,919	53,609	44,005	51,373	61,124

All Academic and Public Libraries

	Mean	First Quartile	Median	Third Quartile
North Atlantic N = 914 Range = $29,615 - $114,919	53,879	45,442	52,300	59,731
Great Lakes & Plains N = 848 Range = $28,745 - $97,800	53,389	46,509	52,435	60,103
Southeast N = 734 Range = $22,500 - $86,528	51,169	42,288	50,576	59,800
West & Southwest N = 993 Range = $21,765 - $95,700	57,639	49,174	57,405	65,793
All Regions N = 3,489 Range = $21,765 - $114,919	54,260	45,780	53,353	61,225

Source: ALA Survey of Librarian Salaries, 2002

MANAGERS/SUPERVISORS OF SUPPORT STAFF
(Page 1 of 3)

Persons who supervise support staff in any part of the library but do not supervise professional librarians.

Medium-sized Public Library
(Serving a population of from 25,000 to 99,999)

	Mean	First Quartile	Median	Third Quartile
North Atlantic N = 110 Range = $26,013 - $74,521	44,178	38,212	42,301	49,676
Great Lakes & Plains N = 161 Range = $19,372 - $65,436	41,215	34,791	40,560	47,778
Southeast N = 56 Range = $22,500 - $45,149	33,583	30,175	32,512	38,739
West & Southwest N = 54 Range = $24,796 - $76,190	43,707	36,827	44,916	51,324
All Regions N = 381 Range = $19,372 - $76,190	41,302	34,568	40,333	47,778

Large Public Library
(Serving a population of 100,000 or more)

	Mean	First Quartile	Median	Third Quartile
North Atlantic N = 291 Range = $22,080 - $83,200	46,388	37,889	45,987	52,690
Great Lakes & Plains N = 318 Range = $22,231 - $72,250	45,397	38,745	44,611	51,636
Southeast N = 316 Range = $22,484 - $82,200	43,340	34,300	40,363	51,370
West & Southwest N = 511 Range = $23,200 - $85,670	45,562	37,601	45,198	50,752
All Regions N = 1,436 Range = $22,080 - $85,670	45,204	36,777	44,619	51,223

Source: ALA Survey of Librarian Salaries, 2002

Managers/Supervisors of support staff (Page 2 of 3)

Persons who supervise support staff in any part of the library but do not supervise professional librarians.

Two-Year College

	Mean	First Quartile	Median	Third Quartile
North Atlantic N = 31 Range = $30,600 - $91,000	53,915	42,000	50,000	63,454
Great Lakes & Plains N = 18 Range = $26,067 - $127,175	46,673	33,355	42,750	52,775
Southeast N = 18 Range = $29,309 - $70,506	38,756	32,875	35,282	40,250
West & Southwest N = 31 Range = $23,346 - $74,829	45,385	34,828	43,644	56,000
All Regions N = 98 Range = $23,346 - $127,175	47,102	35,423	43,734	54,231

Four-Year College

	Mean	First Quartile	Median	Third Quartile
North Atlantic N = 57 Range = $28,000 - $81,040	45,209	36,585	44,016	49,467
Great Lakes & Plains N = 37 Range = $28,000 - $56,390	38,791	32,939	35,237	44,014
Southeast N = 25 Range = $23,100 - $53,730	36,868	31,291	34,800	42,339
West & Southwest N = 16 Range = $25,122 - $44,535	36,374	33,601	35,359	41,890
All Regions N = 135 Range = $23,100 - $81,040	40,858	34,000	40,000	46,350

Source: ALA Survey of Librarian Salaries, 2002

Managers/Supervisors of support staff (Page 3 of 3)

Persons who supervise support staff in any part of the library but do not supervise professional librarians.

University

	Mean	First Quartile	Median	Third Quartile
North Atlantic N = 87 Range = $28,135 - $65,397	45,686	41,100	44,718	50,545
Great Lakes & Plains N = 139 Range = $24,000 - $108,035	46,670	37,817	44,352	52,247
Southeast N = 165 Range = $27,000 - $72,494	42,812	36,745	41,613	48,647
West & Southwest N = 127 Range = $28,292 - $88,416	48,000	37,500	44,040	57,504
All Regions N = 518 Range = $24,000 - $108,035	45,602	37,854	43,092	51,300

All Academic and Public Libraries

	Mean	First Quartile	Median	Third Quartile
North Atlantic N = 576 Range = $22,080 - $91,000	46,148	38,693	44,785	51,804
Great Lakes & Plains N = 673 Range = $19,372 - $127,175	44,330	37,245	43,078	50,465
Southeast N = 580 Range = $22,484 - $82,200	41,827	34,000	39,350	48,600
West & Southwest N = 739 Range = $23,200 - $88,416	45,639	37,044	44,886	51,036
All Regions N = 2,568 Range = $19,372 - $127,175	44,549	36,432	43,211	50,752

Source: ALA Survey of Librarian Salaries, 2002

LIBRARIANS WHO DO NOT SUPERVISE
(Page 1 of 3)

Full-time staff with master's degrees from programs in library and information studies accredited by ALA who were not reported earlier and who do not supervise.

Medium-sized Public Library
(Serving a population of from 25,000 to 99,999)

	Mean	First Quartile	Median	Third Quartile
North Atlantic N = 234 Range = $23,205 - $75,452	43,396	37,028	41,446	48,400
Great Lakes & Plains N = 261 Range = $26,500 - $72,233	39,005	34,639	38,435	42,986
Southeast N = 37 Range = $24,132 - $46,857	33,716	30,488	33,057	35,550
West & Southwest N = 71 Range = $19,574 - $61,620	42,139	36,795	41,688	48,000
All Regions N = 603 Range = $19,574 - $75,452	40,753	35,407	39,577	45,251

Large Public Library
(Serving a population of 100,000 or more)

	Mean	First Quartile	Median	Third Quartile
North Atlantic N = 984 Range = $28,834 - $69,888	41,054	36,834	39,780	44,353
Great Lakes & Plains N = 889 Range = $25,006 - $65,437	42,928	37,666	42,593	46,925
Southeast N = 693 Range = $24,650 - $66,403	39,435	33,670	36,996	45,490
West & Southwest N = 1,248 Range = $27,123 - $75,105	48,620	41,219	48,131	55,740
All Regions N = 3,814 Range = $24,650 - $75,105	43,673	36,834	42,384	49,109

Source: ALA Survey of Librarian Salaries, 2002

Librarians who do not supervise (Page 2 of 3)

Full-time staff with master's degrees from programs in library and information studies accredited by ALA who were not reported earlier and who do not supervise.

Two-Year College

	Mean	First Quartile	Median	Third Quartile
North Atlantic N = 32 Range = $34,500 - $115,721	53,511	41,180	47,221	57,292
Great Lakes & Plains N = 43 Range = $32,000 - $114,477	61,384	48,465	57,000	71,640
Southeast N = 47 Range = $28,000 - $68,467	42,835	34,299	40,160	49,437
West & Southwest N = 43 Range = $29,023 - $98,841	54,003	40,951	50,267	63,993
All Regions N = 165 Range = $28,000 - $115,721	52,650	40,080	48,000	61,635

Four-Year College

	Mean	First Quartile	Median	Third Quartile
North Atlantic N = 55 Range = $24,079 - $86,671	45,468	37,300	43,497	49,712
Great Lakes & Plains N = 32 Range = $32,963 - $58,153	40,757	35,580	39,026	44,206
Southeast N = 22 Range = $25,000 - $43,780	32,610	29,865	31,199	36,297
West & Southwest N = 14 Range = $32,236 - $48,630	39,414	34,287	38,746	43,643
All Regions N = 123 Range = $24,079 - $86,671	41,254	34,280	39,400	45,000

Source: ALA Survey of Librarian Salaries, 2002

Librarians who do not supervise (Page 3 of 3)

Full-time staff with master's degrees from programs in library and information studies accredited by ALA who were not reported earlier and who do not supervise.

University

	Mean	First Quartile	Median	Third Quartile
North Atlantic N = 353 Range = $22,880 - $97,855	46,710	39,000	44,149	50,501
Great Lakes & Plains N = 262 Range = $26,000 - $87,820	44,376	36,980	41,319	48,741
Southeast N = 370 Range = $24,500 - $153,000	42,543	36,153	41,027	47,289
West & Southwest N = 558 Range = $22,252 - $91,973	49,995	39,544	46,964	57,404
All Regions N = 1,543 Range = $22,252 - $153,000	46,502	38,028	43,760	51,996

All Academic and Public Libraries

	Mean	First Quartile	Median	Third Quartile
North Atlantic N = 1,658 Range = $22,880 - $115,721	42,976	36,862	41,389	46,406
Great Lakes & Plains N = 1,487 Range = $25,006 - $114,477	42,981	36,920	42,000	46,892
Southeast N = 1,169 Range = $24,132 - $153,000	40,246	33,670	38,127	46,013
West & Southwest N = 1,934 Range = $19,574 - $98,841	48,832	40,406	48,081	55,740
All Regions N = 6,248 Range = $19,574 - $153,000	44,279	36,905	42,424	49,434

Source: ALA Survey of Librarian Salaries, 2002

Beginning Librarians (Page 3 of 3)

Full-time staff with master's degrees from programs in library and information studies accredited by ALA but no professional experience after receiving the degree.

University

	Mean	First Quartile	Median	Third Quartile
North Atlantic N = 23 Range = $28,000 - $45,000	36,017	34,000	35,000	38,000
Great Lakes & Plains N = 23 Range = $30,500 - $43,000	36,081	32,508	36,000	40,000
Southeast N = 28 Range = $25,000 - $50,000	35,960	32,625	34,000	39,518
West & Southwest N = 34 Range = $28,000 - $65,004	37,670	32,876	36,600	40,000
All Regions N = 108 Range = $25,000 - $65,004	36,536	33,000	35,358	39,000

All Academic and Public Libraries

	Mean	First Quartile	Median	Third Quartile
North Atlantic N = 118 Range = $28,000 - $45,000	34,545	33,850	33,850	34,896
Great Lakes & Plains N = 56 Range = $18,655 - $67,739	34,799	32,173	34,058	36,943
Southeast N = 90 Range = $25,000 - $50,000	32,543	29,403	32,389	33,753
West & Southwest N = 118 Range = $22,521 - $65,004	37,588	34,600	36,700	39,374
All Regions N = 382 Range = $18,655 - $67,739	35,051	32,854	33,850	37,062

Source: ALA Survey of Librarian Salaries, 2002

Discussion

Summary of Results

People interested in a particular type of library or a particular type of work, or a particular region will have their own way of drawing conclusions from the results of this survey. However, the results may be summarized in a very general way by noting that this survey included 14,805 salaries ranging from $18,655 to $200,000 with a mean of $49,866 and a median of $46,600. Another way to summarize is to look at mean salaries paid to particular types of positions, mean salaries paid by particular types of libraries, or mean salaries paid in particular parts of the U.S.

Salaries by Type of Position

The six positions are shown in rank order by mean of salaries paid on Table 1. Also shown is the mean of salaries paid in 2001, the dollar difference and the percent increase.

Table 1. Rank Order of Position Types by Mean of Salaries Paid

Title	2002 Salary	2001 Salary	Change Amount	Percent
Director	75,714	72,384	+3,330	4.6
Deputy/Associate/Assistant Directors	62,847	59,346	+3,501	5.9
Department Heads/Coordinators/Senior Managers	54,260	52,677	+1,583	3.0
Managers/Supervisors of Support Staff	44,549	42,629	+1,920	4.5
Librarians who do not supervise	44,279	42,704	+1,575	3.7
Beginning Librarians	35,051	32,891	+2,160	6.6

SOURCE: ALA SURVEY OF LIBRARIAN SALARIES, 2002

The percentage of increase in the mean of this year's 14,805 salaries over the mean of last year's 13,487 salaries is 4.7 percent. This figure is 1.2% higher than the increase in salaries for all "civilian workers" for the same time period as reported by the U.S. Bureau of Labor Statistics in their Employment Cost Index. The percent change from March 01 to March 02 for civilian workers was 3.5%. The increase for the state and local government subset of civilian workers, which was 3.4%. Data on the Employment Cost Index is published in each issue of the *Monthly Labor Review*, but those figures are now several months behind what can be found on the Web. Percent change figures used in this paragraph were found on July 26, 2002 at: http://www.bls.gov/news.release/eci.t05.htm.

Salaries by Type of Library

For the top two positions, Director/Dean and Deputy/Associate/Assistant Directors salaries were highest in large public libraries and lowest in four-year academic libraries. For the other four categories, salaries were usually highest in two-year academic libraries and lowest in four-year college libraries. For librarians who do not supervise, the mean was lowest in medium-size public libraries.

Salaries by Region of the U.S.
In order to determine which region has the highest salaries, we analyzed the six positions and the five library size/type categories. When the region with the highest mean salary was marked for each position in each size/type category, North Atlantic was checked 56 percent of the time and West and Southwest was highest 40 percent of the time. Great Lakes and Plains was highest once. This pattern is similar to last year, except that in 2002 West and Southwest was the highest more often and North Atlantic was highest less often. The lowest mean salary was in the Southeast 83 percent of the time. Great Lakes and Plains was lowest twice, and West and Southwest was lowest three times. North Atlantic was never lowest and Southeast was never highest.

Problem with Categories New in 1999
There is one problem with the above summary paragraphs, stemming from changes made in the questionnaire in 1999. For libraries in the Association of Research Libraries (ARL), we did not have salaries in two categories: Department Heads/Coordinators/Senior Managers and Managers/Supervisors of Support Staff. We use data already collected by ARL for ARL libraries in our sample, and ARL does not use those two categories. Therefore we knew we do not have salaries in those categories for the 26 ARL libraries in our sample this year. The absence may have an impact on the summaries by type of position and by region.

Complicating Factors

When designing this survey in the early 1980s, we were aware that several aspects of the patterns of employment in libraries would complicate our efforts. As we talked with respondents and users of the reports over the years, we gained additional insights into several factors, which should be taken into consideration when using these results.

The Meaning of "Full-Time"
The questionnaire asked about salaries for **full-time** positions only, but full-time was not defined. There are at least two problems in this area: How many months in a year is full-time? How do you report people who work full-time in the library but part-time at one job and part-time at another?

The months in a year problem primarily affects academic libraries where librarians sometimes have academic year contracts for less than twelve months. In this survey, respondents are asked to indicate the number of months a salary covers and the computer calculated twelve months at the same rate. Appendix G shows how often less-than-twelve-month salaries occur.

The Meaning of "Professional"
In the early years of this survey, respondents were asked to report only salaries paid to professionals, but the word "professional" was not defined. Instead, each position was described in such a way that professional responsibility was clearly implied. Instructions told the respondent to list all incumbents in these positions "regardless of academic credentials." We accepted the judgement of the respondent that the salaries reported were for professional work but found out, when we called about low salaries (see below) that some respondents had doubts about whether a particular incumbent could be described as "professional." When such doubts were expressed, we asked the respondent to make a decision based on the definition in ALA's statement on "Library Education and Personnel Utilization." That policy has since been revised and has a new title, Library and Information Studies Education and Human Resource Utilization". However, the definition relevant here is the same. (See Appendix B, Policy 54.1, Section 8) In 1990, that definition was added to the instructions. Beginning with the 1991 survey, we asked respondents to report only staff *with master's degrees from programs in library and information studies accredited by ALA.*

Salaries Below $22,000
In previous years, this report has described the methodology used to determine the cut-off point below which salaries were investigated as probably not being full-time, professional work. The cut-off point for the 2002 survey was

23

$22,000. Of the 14,827 salaries initially considered usable, 25 were below $22,000 (less than 1%). Staff at the Library Research center used e-mail or telephone to contact the person named as the respondent at the 19 libraries involved. They learned that 22 salaries were for part-time work, were for non-professional positions, or were filled out in error. Those 22 salaries were dropped from the data file used for this report. The dropped salaries had been reported primarily because the respondent had misunderstood the instructions. Once the salaries were dropped, the total usable number of salaries was 14,805. Three (3) salaries of less than $22,000 did remain in the file. Of these, all three were in public libraries.

Job Levels or Faculty Ranks

The wording of this questionnaire is based on an assumption that librarians are compensated at a particular amount for assuming a particular level of responsibility. However, in many libraries that is not true. Some libraries use a system of levels in their compensation structure (e.g., Librarian I, II, III, IV) to account for the background a person brings to a job and the amount of experience the person has. Some academic libraries pay salaries based on faculty rank rather than work done. In many academic libraries where librarians have faculty rank and titles, they are compensated as Instructor, Assistant Professor, Associate Professor or Professor and not as any one of the position categories on our questionnaire. We do not attempt to account for this variety within the structure of our questionnaire.

Several respondents and reviewers of this report have recommended in the past that we collect salary data for librarian levels or ranks. We have considered this seriously, but concluded that it would be at least as confusing as the current method due to the fact that levels and ranks mean different things in different libraries.

Level of Experience

Respondents occasionally ask us to ask for and report salaries in a way that takes into account the years of experience that an incumbent possesses. Unfortunately, providing that information would be a burden on respondents and reporting it would make this report overly complex. This report does take such factors into account in two ways: beginning librarians are reported in a separate table and are not included in salary data for other positions; and data for all positions show figures at the first and third quartile as well as the mean, median, and range.

Appendix A

Compensation Surveys Providing Information on Library Workers

Most library salary surveys listed below are conducted on a regular schedule (annual or biennial) and on a regional or national basis. The library literature should be monitored for reports of one-time surveys by individual libraries or associations. Some state library agencies collect salary and benefits data as part of their ongoing statistical gathering efforts from libraries within their own state. There is wide variation, however, in what data are collected and how these are compiled and reported. Most collect only public library data. Academic and school library data may be collected by other state agencies.

In addition, some state library associations collect salary data, issue recommended salary guidelines, set minimum salaries for professional positions, or publish reports in association journals or newsletters. As of August 2002, nineteen states had established recommended minimum salaries. These include: Connecticut, Delaware, Illinois, Indiana, Iowa, Louisiana, Maine, Massachusetts, New Jersey, North Carolina, Ohio, Pennsylvania, Rhode Island, South Carolina, South Dakota, Texas, Vermont, West Virginia, and Wisconsin. Specific amounts are not listed here because these are updated regularly by the associations. The latest figures can be found in the most recent classified section of *American Libraries* or *College & Research Libraries News*.

A list of state library agency and association addresses can be found in *The Bowker Annual: Library and Book Trade Almanac* or on the Internet at www.dpi.state.wi.us/dpi/dlcl/pld/statelib.html and www.ala.org/cro/state_guide.html respectively.

Individual libraries will sometimes conduct private surveys of institutions of comparable size or in the same geographical area, either through an outside consulting firm or by calling libraries informally. For the most part, these surveys are not published, although the initiating library will often share results with participating libraries. Some library workers are also conducting surveys that compare their salaries with other professions and occupations within their jurisdiction in an effort to achieve pay equity with positions requiring comparable skills, effort, responsibilities and working conditions.

Academic Libraries

Association of Research Libraries. *ARL Annual Salary Survey*. Washington, D.C.: ARL, 1973-.

> The 2001-02 compilation consists of detailed tables of salaries for over 12,000 professional positions based on data collected from ARL member libraries and analyzed by job category, years of experience, sex, minority status, size of library, and geographic region. Included in the publication are tables for general, medical, law, Canadian libraries and non-university research libraries. Information on this survey can be found at www.arl.org/stats/salary/index.html.

To order, contact ARL Publications Distribution Center, PO Box 531, Annapolis Junction, MD 20701-0531, 301/362-8196 (phone), 301/206-9789 (fax), pubs@arl.org (e-mail).

College and University Professional Association for Human Resources. 2001-02 *Administrative Compensation Survey*. Washington, D.C.: CUPA-HR.

The survey includes data on college and university administrative positions from 1,444 public and private institutions. The tables in the survey present the median salary according to institutional budget, enrollment, and classification. Directors of library services are included.

The survey is available from CUPA-HR, 1233 20th St., NW, Suite 301, Washington, D.C. 20035-1250, 202/429-0311 (phone), 202/429-0149 (fax), www.cupahr.org (web); $105 for association members/survey participants, $170 for members/non-participants, $210 for non-members/survey participants and $345 for nonmembers/survey non-participants.

College and University Professional Association for Human Resources. 2001-02 *Mid-Level Administrative/Professional Salary Survey*. Washington, D.C.: CUPA-HR.

This survey features median salary data from 1,135 public and private institutions on 135 positions, including reference specialist, cataloging specialist, Webmaster and other technology based positions. Data are organized by operating budget size and include regional comparisons. $135 for association members/survey participants, $185 for members/non-participants, $230 for nonmembers/survey non-participants. See contact information above.

Public Libraries

American Library Association. Public Library Association. *Public Library Data Service Statistical Report*. Chicago, IL: PLA.

Annual listing with information that includes library-specific salaries for directors and beginning librarians for most public libraries serving 100,000 or more and for many smaller libraries, as well as basic library statistics. The 2002 edition is available from ALA Order Fulfillment, PO Box 932501, Atlanta, GA 31193-2501, 866/746-7252, for $80 with the usual discounts for PLA and ALA members (ISBN 0-8389-1882-8).

Evelina R. Moulder. "Salaries of Municipal Officials, 2001" in *The Municipal Year Book*, 2002. Washington, D.C.: International City/County Management Association.

Chief librarian salaries for local public libraries are included with earnings of other city department heads. These are reported by geographic region, population size, city type (i.e., central, suburban, independent) and form of government. The mean, median, and first and third quartiles are included for libraries serving ten different population groups ranging from under 2,500 to over 1,000,000. *The Municipal Year Book* is published in April of each year and includes salary data from the previous year. To order, call 800-745-8780.

Sandstedt, Carl R. *Salary Survey: West-North-Central States.* St. Peters, Mo.: St. Charles City-County Library.

This annual survey provides data for directors, assistant directors, department heads, starting MLS, and several support positions for public libraries in West-North-Central States (North Dakota, South Dakota, Nebraska, Kansas, Minnesota, Iowa, Missouri). Average salaries are presented by size of library budget. Also includes per FTE costs, per capita support, and per capita materials budget.

St. Charles City-County Library District, 425 Spencer Rd., Box 529, St. Peters, MO 63376. Available online at www.win.org/library/.

School Libraries

Educational Research Service. *Salaries and Wages for Professional and Support Personnel in Public Schools*, Arlington, VA: ERS, 2001-02.

ERS publishes an annual report of salaries for public school personnel, which includes data for school librarians and library clerks. The report covers scheduled salaries for professional personnel and actual salaries paid for professional and support personnel by enrollment group, per pupil expenditure, and geographic region. It also includes year-to-year, five-year, and ten-year information on trends in public school salaries and wages, with comparisons to the Consumer Price Index for each of these periods. The report costs $150 (call for subscriber prices). Available from ERS, 2000 Clarendon Blvd., Arlington, VA 22201, 703/243-2100.

Marilyn L. Miller and Marilyn L. Shontz. "Expenditures for Resources in School Library Media Centers." *School Library Journal*.

As part of a report every two years on budgets for and expenditures by school library media centers, some median and mean salary data for media specialists are reported by level of school. Included are comparisons of schools with and without district level library media coordinators. *School Library Journal*, 245 W. 17th St., New York, NY 10011, 212/463-6759.

National Education Association. *Rankings and Estimates of School Statistics*. Washington, D.C.: NEA, 2001-02.

NEA's annual report of current, state-level education data includes sources of school revenue, teacher salaries, and per-pupil expenditure.

For further information, contact NEA Professional Library, PO Box 2035, Annapolis Junction,

MD 20701-2035, 800-229-4200 (phone), 301/206-9789 (fax).

Specialized Libraries

American Association of Law Libraries. *Biennial Salary Survey 2001*. Chicago, IL: AALL.

The report summarizes salary information for law libraries with three following sections that cover academic libraries, private firm/corporate libraries and state, court and county libraries. The data is broken out and crossed-tabbed by position, region, gender, education, years in current position and years of library experience and further by geographical regions in the U.S.

The price for the publication is $95 for AALL members, $150 for nonmembers (includes shipping). Contact AALL, 53 W. Jackson Blvd., Suite 940, Chicago, IL 60604, 312/939-4764 (phone), 312/431-1097 (fax), www.aallnet.org (web). (AALL members may browse the online edition free of charge.)

Association of Academic Health Sciences Libraries. *Annual Statistics of Medical School Libraries in the United States and Canada*. Seattle, WA: AAHSLD, 2001-02.

Salaries are provided for director, associate director, division head, department head, other librarians, and entry-level positions. Minimum, maximum and mean are provided for the positions and arranged by region.

It's available at a no cost to members of AAHSL and $250 for nonmembers. The current edition and previous editions may be ordered by contacting AAHSL, 2150 N. 107th St., #205, Seattle, WA 98133, 206/367-8704 (phone), 206/367-8777 (fax), www.aahsl.org (web).

Medical Library Association. *Health Sciences Librarian Compensation: Results of MLA's 2001 Salary Survey*. Chicago: MLA, 2001.

More than 1,900 members provided data for the 2001 triennial salary survey, available in summary format to MLA's members via the association's website, www.mlanet.org. The summary offers detailed information by job title, geographical area, type of institution, and more. Contact Kate Corcoran, MLA, 65 E. Wacker Pl., Suite 1900, Chicago, IL 60601-7298, 312/419-9094, ext. 12.

Special Libraries Association. *SLA Annual Salary Survey*. Washington, D.C.: SLA, 2002.

Salaries are reported at the 25th, 50th (median) and 75th percentiles and contain breakdowns by industry, geographic region, administrative responsibility, sex, education level, and experience. Data for the U.S. and Canada are presented in separate tables.

The Salary Survey is a comprehensive report containing the most accurate U.S. and Canadian salary information gathered by a member survey. A wide variety of variables are covered including industry type, geographical area, job title, budget range and years of experience.

The report, available in late fall to SLA members for $45, $125 non-members. Contact Special Libraries Association, 1700 18th St., N.W., Washington, D.C. 20009-2514, 202/939-3673 (phone), 202/234-4700 (fax).

Other

Association for Library and Information Science Education. *ALISE Statistical Report and Database.* Reston, VA: ALISE, 1980-.

Average and median salaries for faculty and administrators in 56 ALISE member schools are provided in this annual report by sex, rank and term of appointment.

Back issues (1981-) of the report are available from ALISE, 11250 Roger Bacon Dr., #8, Reston, VA 20190-5202, 703/234-4146 (phone), 703/435-4390 (fax), alise@drohanmgmt.com (e-mail). Current issue is $65 (non-members), including postage and handling (U.S. funds), $35 for members. This annual report is published in the summer.

College and University Professional Association for Human Resources. 2001-02 *National Faculty Salary Survey by Discipline and Rank in Private Four-Year Colleges and Universities.* Washington, D.C.: CUPA-HR.

College and University Professional Association for Human Resources. 2001-02 *National Faculty Salary Survey by Discipline and Rank in Public Four-Year Colleges and Universities.* Washington, D.C.: CUPA-HR.

Annual surveys collect data for five faculty ranks in 80 disciplines and major fields. A total of 519 private and 352 public institutions participated in the most recent study. Communications, Communication Technologies, Computer Information Sciences, and Library Sciences are included. The listings are for those who teach in library science programs, not those who hold faculty rank as academic librarians. Faculty Salary Surveys are each $80 for survey participants, $110 non-participant, CUPA-HR members; and $135 for non-participants, nonmembers from CUPA-HR, 1233 20th St., NW, Suite 301, Washington, D.C. 20036-1250, 202/429-0311 (phone), 202/429-0149 (fax), www.cupahr.org (web).

"Placements and Salaries 2001." *Library Journal.*

An annual survey since 1951 of ALA-accredited library and information studies education programs (usually published in the October 15th issue of *Library Journal* with data from previous calendar year.) For each reporting school, the low, high, average and median salaries are reported for men, women, and total placements. This information is also provided for five regions of the U.S. An additional table shows the distribution of high, low, average and median salaries by type of library for men, women and total placements.

Employee Benefits

Although some states collect data on employee benefits, little information is collected on a regional or national level on a regular basis for library workers.

PROVIDENCE Associates, Inc. *Public Library Work Benefits Survey*. Denton, TX: 1997.

> Results of a survey of 25 public libraries in 1997 provides salary ranges and average salaries for 5 staff levels, plus data on vacation days, sick leave, leave of absence, pension plans, health and life insurance, and other benefits. Single copies available for $10.00 plus $2.50 shipping/handling, from PROVIDENCE Associates, Inc., 488 Mill Dr., 2nd floor, Cottonwood, AZ 86326-5340, aneyeforit@sedona.net. Look for the next survey in Spring 2003.

Salary Surveys for Other Library Workers and Related Information Professionals

For salary data on other types of workers that may be employed in libraries, the following surveys might be useful:

Abbott, Langer and Associates, Inc., Dept NET, 548 First St., Crete, IL 60417, 708/672-4200 (phone), www.abbott-langer.com (web). Conducts annual or biennial salary surveys for the following fields: legal and related jobs in business and industry; industrial engineers; plant and facilities managers and engineers; consulting engineering firms; consulting firms; independent lab/testing/inspection firms; geologists; human resources/personnel department; service department; nonprofit organizations; research and development; manufacturing; food and beverage processing; security/loss prevention dept.; MIS/data processing; accounting departments; accounting firms; advertising agencies; sales/marketing management; direct marketing; life sciences and telecommunications.

> *Compensation in Nonprofit Organizations* contains information on salaries of Directors of Information with this type of employer. Mean, median, first and third quartile, and first and ninth decile data, salary ranges, current salaries, and total compensation (salaries plus bonuses) are reported by supervisory responsibility, type of nonprofit organization, total annual budget, geographic scope of organization, number of employees, region, state, and metropolitan area, and type of organization vs. remaining variables.

> *Available Pay Survey Reports: An Annotated Bibliography* (6th ed.) by Dr. Steven Langer (2002) contains annotations of over 1,200 pay survey reports, both domestic and foreign. Annotations are indexed by source, geographic area, type of employer, and job title/function/college curricula.

The *Library Mosaics*, a bi-monthly magazine for support staff in libraries, media and information centers has published the "Library Support Staff Salary Survey" by Charlie Fox and Raymond Roney in the July/August 2000 issue. It provides a general overview of support staff. *Library Mosaics*, PO Box 5171, Culver City, CA 90231, 310/645-4998 (phone), editor@librarymosaics.com (e-mail).

The AMS Foundation Business Survey Group, PO Box 26644, Milwaukee, WI 53226, 800/229-5655, artwelch@msn.com. Conducts surveys of office/clerical, secretarial/administrative, professional, data processing and middle management jobs as well as pertinent business trends. Available is the 2002 edition of the *Office/Clerical, Secretarial/Administrative, Professional, Data Processing and Management Survey*. Also available is the *Business Expenses and New Benefits, Contract Labor, Flexible Work, Internet Usage, Telecommuting, Training and Relocation*, and *Travel Expenses* report.

Datamation publishes an annual salary survey of computer and information systems personnel. The magazine reports on average salaries for positions in systems analysis, programming, database administration, data entry, office automation, and computer operations, by industry and regions. Results are based on averages or totals from the following information: salary, job type, job skills, and location, http://datamation.earthweb.com/.

U.S. Department of Labor, Bureau of Labor Statistics, National Compensation Survey program produces information on wages by occupation for many metropolitan areas and also for the nation as a whole. It provides data on occupational earnings, employer costs for wages, salaries, and benefits, and details of employer-provided benefit and establishment practices. This umbrella program combines the Occupational Compensation Surveys, the Employment Cost Index, and the Employee Benefits Survey and is published annually. For further information call 202/691-6199, or visit URL http://stats.bls.gov/ncs/.

Appendix B

ALA Policies Relating to Salary Issues

The following are policies endorsed by the ALA Council and included in the "ALA Policy Manual" which appears annually in the *ALA Handbook of Organization*.

Policy #54.1 Library and Information Studies Education and Human Resource Utilization

8. The title "Librarian" carries with it the connotation of "professional" in the sense that professional tasks are those which require a special background and education on the basis of which library needs are identified, problems are analyzed, goals are set, and original and creative solutions are formulated for them, integrating theory into practice, and planning, organizing, communicating, and administering successful programs of service to users of the library's materials and services. In defining services to users, the professional person recognizes potential users as well as current ones, and designs services, which will reach all who could benefit from them.

9. The title "Librarian" therefore should be used only to designate positions in libraries, which utilize the qualifications and impose the responsibilities suggested above. Positions which are primarily devoted to the routine application of established rules and techniques, however useful and essential to the effective operation of a library's ongoing services, should not carry the word "Librarian" in the job title.

11. The salaries for each category should offer a range of promotional steps sufficient to permit a career-in-rank. The top salary in any category should overlap the beginning salary in the next higher category, in order to give recognition to the value of experience and knowledge gained on the job.

18. The first professional category—Librarian or Specialist—assumes responsibilities that are professional in the sense described in paragraph #8 above. A well-rounded liberal education plus graduate-level study in the field of specialization (either in librarianship or in a relevant field) are seen as the minimum preparation for the kinds of assignments implied. The title, however, is given for a position entailing professional responsibilities and not automatically upon achievement of the academic degree.

19. The Senior categories assume relevant professional experience as well as qualifications beyond those required for admission to the first professional ranks. Normally, it is assumed that such advanced qualification shall be held in some specialty, either in a particular aspect of librarianship or some relevant subject field. Subject specializations are as applicable in the Senior Librarian category as they are in the Senior Specialist category.

20. Administrative responsibilities entail high-level specialty, and appointment to positions in top administration should normally require the qualifications of Senior Librarian with a specialization in administration. This category, however, is not limited to administrators, whose specialty is only one of several specializations of value to the library service. There are many areas of special knowledge within librarianship which are equally important and to which equal recognition in

prestige and salary should be given. Highly qualified persons with specialist responsibilities in some aspects of librarianship—archives, bibliography, reference, for example—should be eligible for advanced status and financial rewards without being forced to abandon for administrative responsibilities their areas of major competence.

Policy #54.4 Comparable Rewards

The American Library Association supports salary administration, which gives reasonable and comparable recognition to positions having administrative, technical, subject, and linguistic requirements. It is recognized that all such specialist competencies can be intellectually vigorous and meet demanding professional operational needs. In administering such a policy, it can be a useful guide that, in major libraries, as many non-administrative specialties be assigned to the top classifications, as are administrative staff. Whenever possible there should be as many at the top rank with less than 30 percent administrative load as there are at the highest rank carrying over 70 percent administrative load.

Policy #54.7 Security of Employment for Library Employees

Security of employment, as an elementary right, guarantees specifically.....a sufficient degree of economic security to make employment in the library attractive to men and women of ability.

Policy #54.8 The Library's Pay Plan

Libraries should have a well constructed and well-administered pay plan based on systematic analysis and evaluation of jobs in the library and which will assure equal pay for equal work. (Note: For text of full statement, see the end of this section.)

Policy #54.9 Permanent Part-Time Employment

The right to earn a living includes a right to part-time employment on a par with full-time employment, including prorated pay and fringe benefits, opportunity for advancement and protection of tenure, access to middle and upper level jobs, and exercise of full responsibilities at any level.

ALA shall create more voluntarily chosen upgraded permanent part-time jobs in its own organization and supports similar action on the part of all libraries.

Policy #54.10 Equal Opportunity and Salaries

The American Library Association supports and works for the achievement of equal salaries and opportunity for employment and promotion for men and women.

The Association fully supports the concept of comparable wages for comparable work that aims at levels of pay for female-oriented occupations equal to those of male-oriented occupations; ALA therefore supports all legal and legislative efforts to achieve wages for library workers commensurate with wages in other occupations with similar qualifications, training, and responsibilities.

ALA particularly supports the efforts of those library workers who have documented, and are legally challenging, the practice of discriminatory salaries, and whose success will benefit all library workers throughout the nation.

Policy #54.11 Collective Bargaining

The American Library Association recognizes the principle of collective bargaining as one of the methods of conducting labor-management relations used by private and public institutions. The Association affirms the right of eligible library employees to organize and bargain collectively with their employers, or to refrain from organizing and bargaining collectively, without fear of reprisal.

Policy #54.18 Advertising Salary Ranges

Available ranges shall be given for positions listed in any placement services provided by ALA and its units. A regional salary guide delineating the latest minimum salary figures recommended by state library associations shall be made available from any placement services provided by ALA and its units. All ALA and unit publications printing classified job advertisements shall include a regional salary guide delineating the latest minimum salary figures recommended by state library association for library positions.

Full Text of Policy # 54.8: The Library's Pay Plan*

The American Library Association believes that an important factor in establishing and maintaining good library service is adequate pay for library employees as exemplified in a well-constructed and well-administered pay plan. A knowledge of the principles on which sound salary administration is based must be the foundation of an equitable pay plan. To aid the library's governing board, its administration, and its staff in the formulation, promulgation, and operation of such a pay plan, the ALA Board on Personnel Administration sets forth in a series of related statements the principles of salary planning and administration.

1. A sound pay plan will be predicated on a systematic analysis and evaluation of jobs in the library, and will reflect the current organization and objectives of the library, recognizing different levels of difficulty and responsibility inherent in various positions, whether these are classified as professional, nonprofessional, administrative, specialist, maintenance, or trade; the relationship among positions in terms of difficulty and responsibility will thus be expressed in a unified plan which will integrate all types of service and will assure equal pay for equal work.

2. An equitable salary schedule will be provided for each class of position that is comparable to that received by persons employed in analogous work in the area and required to have analogous training and qualifications.

The salaries of nonprofessional employees, maintenance and skilled trade workers employed by the library system will compare with those of local workers performing similar duties. The salary schedules for professional library positions, in the case of the community where the pay scale does not meet competing rates outside, may need to exceed the prevailing local level for other professional personnel. Since the recruiting of professionally trained librarians is on a nation-wide basis, the library system must compete with rates paid in the country as a whole in order to obtain and retain a high quality of professional personnel. In libraries in educational institutions (elementary, secondary, and higher education) the professional librarians will normally be on the faculty pay plan, with the salary schedules of the various classes of faculty rank adjusted to compensate equitably for such factors as shorter vacations and longer work week; where a separate pay plan is used, it will be comparable with that of the faculty and adjusted to compensate equitably for such factors as vacation and work week.

3. An equitable salary schedule will provide for each class of position a minimum and a maximum salary and a series of increments within each salary range, such increments to be granted on the basis of demonstrated competence, individual development (whether through growth on the job or through formal education), and attitude.

*Note: This policy was passed by the ALA Council in July 1955. It still remains a useful statement regarding the administration of a library's pay plan. Readers should note, however, that the references to the Board on Personnel Administration are not applicable since this unit is no longer in existence

4. The library system in developing a pay plan, and in reviewing it to maintain its adequacy, will identify one or more key positions in the professional and in the other services, set salary schedules for these positions which are comparable to prevailing rates for such positions, and develop and adjust the salary schedule for other levels of positions in relation to the salary schedules set for each of these key positions.

5. The pay plan ladder consisting of the salary schedules for the various classes of positions will provide an orderly progression from the lowest to the highest schedule, with each schedule reflecting properly the difference in level of duties and responsibilities of positions in that classification from those in the schedule below and above it but without wide gaps or serious overlapping between schedules.

6. An equitable pay plan will reflect living costs in the community, the cost of maintaining an appropriate level of living, and the ability of the jurisdiction to pay for the service.

7. All policies and rules concerning the operation and administration of the pay plan will be set forth clearly in writing and will accompany the pay plan.

8. Though final approval and adoption of the pay plan and rules for its operation rest with the governing board and administration of the library, it is desirable that the library staff participates in the formulation of both the plan and its operating rules.

9. Each staff member will be informed of the salary schedule for his or her class of position, of the relation of that schedule to the pay plan as a whole, and of the policies and rules governing the operation of the plan.

The current studies of the ALA Board on Personnel Administration giving salary data for key positions will provide useful material for the library system in developing and maintaining the adequacy of its pay plan.

Appendix C

Technical Considerations

Formation of Library Groups

As in previous years, the survey samples were selected from two library universes – public and academic. The public library universe included all public libraries serving populations of 25,000 or more and was stratified into two classes – those serving populations of from 25,000 to 99,999 and those serving populations of 100,000 or more.

The academic library universe was stratified into three categories: two-year college, four-year college, and university using the 1998 Academic Library Survey file. This file includes codes for the categories created by the Carnegie Foundation for the Advancement of Teaching in 1994. Our "two-year college" corresponds to the Carnegie category "Associate of Arts." Our "four-year college" category corresponds to the Carnegie Categories "Baccalaureate I and II." Our "university" includes the Carnegie categories "Master's I and II, Doctoral I and II, and Research I and II."

Within each of these five strata, libraries were furthered stratified into four geographic areas used frequently by National Center for Education Statistics (NCES): North Atlantic, Great Lakes and Plains, Southeast, West, and Southwest. A list of states included in each region is provided in Table D-1. As in previous surveys, the five library classes and four geographic areas were combined to form twenty groups from which samples were selected. Tables D2-D7 show the size of each group, the size of the sample, and the size of the return.

Sample Selection and Return

The size of the sample for each type/size/geographic strata was determined by using a proportional sampling procedure that took into account the size of the population in each group and the expected return rate for the survey. The public library sample was selected using a file from the NCES containing 1998 data on all public libraries submitted to NCES by state library agencies as part of the Federal State Cooperative System for Public Library Data (FSCS). This file includes data on the number of staff with master's degrees from programs in library and information studies accredited by ALA. Before selecting the sample, LRC dropped from the sampling frame libraries that did not have at least two of such personnel and libraries that had refused to respond in the years from 1990 through 2001 for reasons that seemed unlikely to change.

The procedure for selecting the academic library sample was similar to the procedure followed in previous years. The Library Research Center (LRC) created a sampling frame by using the universe file described above (see second paragraph). This file includes data on the number of staff who are "librarians and other professionals". Before selecting the sample, LRC dropped from the sampling frame libraries that did not have at least two of such personnel and libraries that had refused to respond in the years from 1990 through 2001 for reasons that seemed unlikely to change. Then LRC screened out several sets of institutions. Removed were institutions with fewer than two full-time professionals and institutions categorized as "specialized" by the Carnegie Corporation for the Advancement of Teaching. Those institutions offer degrees ranging from the bachelor's to the doctorate, at least 50 percent of which are in a single specialized field, e.g., "theological seminaries, Bible colleges, and other institutions offering degrees in religion," and "Schools of art, music, and design." Specialized institutions often declined to respond in the early years of this survey. Also excluded were four sets of institutions whose individual members had been unable to respond in the past. In New York, the seventeen institutions that are part of the City University of New York were removed because librarians there have full academic status and salary is not related to position description. Public two-year schools in

California were removed for the same reason, as were the fourteen members of the state university system in Pennsylvania. Also in Pennsylvania, we removed all but the main campus of Pennsylvania State University because librarians at other campuses declined to respond in the past and referred us to the main campus.

In addition to the 924 returns analyzed for this report, we also received 15 returns that could not be used. They fell into the following categories:

- Seven were from libraries where none of the staff are full-time or none of the full-time staff had master's degrees from programs in library and information studies accredited by ALA.

- Five refused for various reasons. Two of these were from academic libraries where salary data are confidential by institutional policy. Three were from academic libraries where the salary structure did not fit our survey.

- Three were from academic institutions that are now closed.

Procedure

The questionnaire and cover letter were mailed on April 11, 2002. A postage-paid business reply envelope was enclosed to encourage response. A second mailing was sent to all non-respondents in May. A third mailing was sent in June only to non-respondents in several strata where response was under 70 percent. Questionnaires were returned to the Library Research Center (LRC) of the University of Illinois Graduate School of Library and Information Science, where they were coded, entered into a data file, cleaned, and analyzed using SPSS for Windows.

Again this year a special procedure was followed for libraries that are members of the Association of Research Libraries (ARL). ARL, which includes about 100 of the largest university libraries in the U.S., conducts its own annual salary survey. Data are gathered for salaries as of July 1 and published the following spring. ARL libraries are also included in the sample for the ALA survey. In the past, some have declined to answer because they are unable to spend time completing another salary questionnaire. For the 2002 survey, ARL again agreed to cooperate with us to save work for everyone. After the sample was selected, we identified the ARL libraries on the list and sent the directors a special mailing asking them to release salaries already on file with ARL. Twenty-six of the twenty-nine ARL libraries in the sample agreed to release data. We sent ARL a list of the ARL position codes that matched the position descriptions in our questionnaire and ARL sent salary data to LRC electronically for those positions in the selected institutions. These salaries were entered into the data file along with salaries reported on the questionnaire.

This procedure worked well and saved time both in the libraries involved and in survey processing. It has two drawbacks, however. ARL does not specify that salaries should be reported only for staff with master's degrees from programs in library and information studies accredited by ALA and some ARL libraries include "other professionals" as well as librarians. For the most part, however, we expect that those "other professionals" are in the ARL position code of "Functional Specialist" which was *not* on the list of codes we requested from ARL. Also, the ARL survey does not ask respondents to indicate the type of staff supervised which is the key distinction between two categories in the ALA survey: Department Heads/Coordinators/Senior Managers and Managers/Supervisors of Support Staff. Because we are aware of the burden it will place on ARL libraries to ask them to complete the new questionnaire, we decided to use as much data as we could from ARL and accept the fact that salaries at ARL libraries are not included for the two positions just noted.

Table C-1. States in Four Regions of the U.S.

North Atlantic	Great Lakes and Plains	Southeast	West and Southwest
Connecticut	Illinois	Alabama	Alaska
Delaware	Indiana	Arkansas	Arizona
District of Columbia	Iowa	Florida	California
Maine	Kansas	Georgia	Colorado
Maryland	Michigan	Kentucky	Hawaii
Massachusetts	Minnesota	Louisiana	Idaho
New Hampshire	Missouri	Mississippi	Montana
New Jersey	Nebraska	North Carolina	Nevada
New York	North Dakota	South Carolina	New Mexico
Pennsylvania	Ohio	Tennessee	Oklahoma
Rhode Island	South Dakota	Virginia	Oregon
Vermont	Wisconsin	West Virginia	Texas
			Utah
			Washington
			Wyoming

SOURCE: STATISITCS OF PUBLIC LIBRARIES, 1977-1978 (NCES, 1982)

Table C-2. Medium-Sized Public Libraries: Size of Group, Sample, Return

	GROUP	SAMPLE		RETURN	
	#	#	% of Group	#	% of Sample
North Atlantic	325	123	37.8	87	70.7
Great Lakes and Plains	319	121	37.9	89	73.6
Southeast	184	70	38.0	47	67.1
West and Southwest	188	71	37.8	56	78.9
TOTAL	1,016	385	37.9	279	72.5

Table C-3. Large Public Libraries: Size of Group, Sample, Return

	GROUP	SAMPLE		RETURN	
	#	#	% of Group	#	% of Sample
North Atlantic	64	58	90.6	41	70.7
Great Lakes and Plains	93	57	62.3	46	80.7
Southeast	132	62	50.0	51	82.3
West and Southwest	160	81	50.6	61	75.3
TOTAL	449	258	57.5	199	77.1

Table C-4. Two-Year College Libraries: Size of Group, Sample, Return

	GROUP	SAMPLE		RETURN	
	#	#	% of Group	#	% of Sample
North Atlantic	133	46	34.6	28	60.9
Great Lakes and Plains	135	46	34.1	25	54.3
Southeast	205	65	31.7	39	60.0
West and Southwest	154	49	31.8	30	61.2
TOTAL	627	206	32.9	122	59.2

Table C-5. Four-Year College Libraries: Size of Group, Sample, Return

	GROUP	SAMPLE		RETURN	
	#	#	% of Group	#	% of Sample
North Atlantic	82	46	56.1	33	71.7
Great Lakes and Plains	90	46	51.1	30	65.2
Southeast	93	46	49.5	29	63.0
West and Southwest	25	25	100.0	14	56.0
TOTAL	290	163	56.2	106	65.0

Table C-6. University Libraries: Size of Group, Sample, Return

	GROUP	SAMPLE		RETURN	
	#	#	% of Group	#	% of Sample
North Atlantic	267	85	31.8	51	60.0
Great Lakes and Plains	250	78	31.2	54	69.2
Southeast	233	74	31.8	58	78.4
West and Southwest	225	71	31.6	55	77.5
TOTAL	975	308	31.6	218	70.8

Table C-7. All Libraries Surveyed: Size of Group, Sample, Return

	GROUP	SAMPLE		RETURN	
	#	#	% of Group	#	% of Sample
North Atlantic	871	358	41.1	240	67.0
Great Lakes and Plains	887	348	39.2	244	70.1
Southeast	847	317	37.4	224	70.7
West and Southwest	752	297	39.5	216	72.7
TOTAL	3,357	1,320	39.3	924	70.0

Appendix D

50 East Huron Street
Chicago, Illinois 60611-2795
USA

Telephone 312 944 6180
Fax 312 440 9374
TDD 312 944 7298
E-mail: ala@ala.org
http://www.ala.org

ALAAmericanLibraryAssocation

April 12, 2002

Dear Colleague:

ALA needs your help in providing information to the library community. The enclosed survey concerns salaries paid to librarians with master's degrees from programs in library and information studies accredited by ALA who hold full-time positions in academic and public libraries. Your institution has been selected as part of a random sample of libraries to receive the enclosed questionnaire. Only summary results will be reported; individual responses will not be identified.

ALA collected and published similar information biennially from 1982 to 1988, and annually since 1989. The results of these surveys have been useful to librarians applying for positions, to librarians setting salaries, and to many others interested in the compensation of librarians. If you have completed this survey before, please note that the categories are somewhat different. Beginning with the 1999 survey, the categories focus on the nature of responsibility for the work of other staff.

Because your library is one of a scientifically selected sample, your response is essential to the success of the survey. As an indication of our thanks for your help, all participants are entitled to a 25% discount on the price of the report. (Mention this entitlement when you place an order. The report will be published in September, 2002.) If your staff is very large and this form is difficult to use, please contact Mary Jo Lynch using one of the methods given below. We want your response and will work with you to make use of whatever data you can provide.

Please complete the questionnaire and return it in the enclosed self-addressed, postage-paid envelope. Please return it as soon as possible, but no later than May 3, 2002. If you have questions about the survey, please contact Mary Jo Lynch, Director, ALA Office for Research and Statistics at 1-800-545-2433, ext. 1-4273 or mlynch@ala.org.

Thank you very much for your cooperation.

Sincerely yours,

William R. Gordon
Executive Director
American Library Association

WRG/kdb

P.S. In order to ensure the validity of the survey results, reminders will be sent to nonrespondents. However, we would rather spend the postage money on other services. Please help our budget by returning this form promptly.

Appendix E

AMERICAN LIBRARY ASSOCIATION
SURVEY OF LIBRARIAN SALARIES, 2002

- This survey requests annual salaries paid to full-time professional librarians, i.e., persons who have master's degrees from programs in library and information studies accredited by the ALA.

- It is our expectation that each full-time professional librarian on your library's staff will fit into one of the six categories on this survey. Therefore, salaries for all full-time professional librarians should be reported.

- Please report the actual salary paid to each full-time person in the categories below as of April 1, 2002. Do not include benefits.

- If it is easier for you to use separate sheets of paper or attach a computer printout, please feel free to do so. Also, if you have more employees than the number of spaces provided in a given section, please list additional salaries on a separate piece of paper, and label it with the appropriate category from the survey form.

- If two or more persons in a category have the same annual salary, you need not write the salary more than once. **Instead** indicate the number of persons receiving the particular amount. (e.g., 2@$37,500).

SPECIAL NOTE FOR ACADEMIC LIBRARIES:

- If an incumbent is considered full-time but works LESS than a 12-month year (including vacation), please report the salary and circle the appropriate number of months (9 or 10) for which the salary is paid. The numbers are on the form to the right of each salary line.

- If services are contributed (i.e., institution pays some expenses or an honorarium but not a true salary), please do not list the incumbent.

PART I. SALARIES PAID TO BEGINNING LIBRARIANS

In the last six months did you hire, for full-time work, one or more persons who have master's degrees from programs in library and information studies accredited by ALA but no professional experience after receiving the degree?

                    Yes   1 (PLEASE LIST ANNUAL SALARIES BELOW)

                    No   2 (PLEASE CONTINUE THE SURVEY)

1 _____ 9/10   3 _____ 9/10   5 _____ 9/10   7 _____ 9/10

2 _____ 9/10   4 _____ 9/10   6 _____ 9/10   8 _____ 9/10

Note: Do not repeat these salaries elsewhere on this form.

PART II. SALARIES PAID TO EXPERIENCED LIBRARIANS

Director/Dean*:

List salary of chief officer of the library or library system.

Annual Salary _____ 9/10

* Report only full-time staff *with master's degrees from programs in library and information studies accredited by ALA*.

Deputy/Associate/Assistant Director :*

List annual salaries of persons who report to the Director and manage major aspects of the library operation (e.g., technical services, public services, collection development, systems/automation).

1_____9_____10   3_____9_____10   5_____9_____10   7_____9_____10

2_____9_____10   4_____9_____10   6_____9_____10   8_____9_____10

Department Heads/Coordinators/Senior Managers:*

List annual salaries of persons who supervise one or more professional librarians*.

1_____9_____10   6_____9_____10   11_____9_____10   16_____9_____10

2_____9_____10   7_____9_____10   12_____9_____10   17_____9_____10

3_____9_____10   8_____9_____10   13_____9_____10   18_____9_____10

4_____9_____10   9_____9_____10   14_____9_____10   19_____9_____10

5_____9_____10   10_____9_____10   15_____9_____10   20_____9_____10

Managers/Supervisors of support staff:*

List annual salaries of persons who supervise support staff in any part of the library but do <u>not</u> supervise professional librarians.

1_____9_____10   5_____9_____10   9_____9_____10   13_____9_____10

2_____9_____10   6_____9_____10   10_____9_____10   14_____9_____10

3_____9_____10   7_____9_____10   11_____9_____10   15_____9_____10

4_____9_____10   8_____9_____10   12_____9_____10   16_____9_____10

* Report only full-time staff *with master's degrees from programs in library and information studies accredited by ALA*. Do not repeat salaries from Part 1.

Librarians who do not supervise:

List annual salaries of full-time staff with master's degrees from programs in library and information studies accredited by ALA who were not reported earlier and who have no supervisory responsibilities.

1_____9_____10	7_____9_____10	13_____9_____10	19_____9_____10
2_____9_____10	8_____9_____10	14_____9_____10	20_____9_____10
3_____9_____10	9_____9_____10	15_____9_____10	21_____9_____10
4_____9_____10	10_____9_____10	16_____9_____10	22_____9_____10
5_____9_____10	11_____9_____10	17_____9_____10	23_____9_____10
6_____9_____10	12_____9_____10	18_____9_____10	24_____9_____10

Part III - Supplementary Questions

Because of recent publicity about the shortage of librarians, ALA is often asked questions such as: How many positions are vacant at any one point in time? Do vacancies exist equally in all regions? What are the main reasons why positions are hard to fill? Your answers to the following questions will help us respond to those inquiries.

1. As of April 1, 2002, are there any full-time MLS positions for which funding is available that are vacant in your library? **(Circle the appropriate number)**

    Yes 1
    No **(Skip to Question 5)**........... 2

2. How many full-time MLS positions are now vacant? **Report only funded positions**.

    _____ vacant positions

3. Of the number reported above, how many have been vacant for six months or more?

    _____ positions vacant six months or more

PLEASE CONTINUE

4. Please consider the following list of reasons why the position(s) reported in Questions 3 is (are) still vacant, select up to three as the most likely. **(Circle the appropriate numbers)**

   Low salaries at your institution 1

   High cost of living in the area 2

   Geographic location of library.. 3

   Lack of MLS degree holders generally.. 4

   Shortage of people with particular specialty (e.g., children, science, technical services).. 5

   Lack of technical expertise 6

   Lack of management expertise.. 7

   Other **(please specify)**... 8

   _____

5. Have the events of September 11th caused a reduction in the numbers of funded positions vacant in your library? **(Circle the appropriate number)**

   Yes.. 1
   No... 2

Name and title of respondent*: _____

Telephone number: _____

Fax Number: _____   **E-mail address:** _____

* Neither libraries nor individuals will be identified in the report of this survey. The name of your library is given on the last page so that we can avoid sending reminders to libraries that respond. The name, phone, fax, and email address of the person responding are requested because we may need to contact him or her if we have questions about this return.

THANK YOU VERY MUCH! *Please return by May 3, 2002 in the enclosed postage paid envelope. If you lose the reply envelope, please send the form to:*

Library Research Center
University of Illinois at Urbana-Champaign
501 East Daniel Street
Champaign Illinois 61820

Appendix F

Salaries Paid for Less Than a Twelve Month Year in Academic Libraries

Instructions on the questionnaire told the respondent: If the incumbent works **less** than a 12-month year (including vacation), please report the salary and circle the appropriate number of months (9 or 10) for which the salary is paid. A program was written to prorate these salaries to their twelve month equivalents for the purpose of reporting results of this survey. Table F was created to show how often this process was necessary. The first column shows the total from tables in this 2002 report. The second column shows how many were reported as being for nine months and the third column shows the percentage of incumbents in the category (position/type of library) which that number represents. The following columns repeat that pattern for positions reported as being for ten months and then for a combination of nine and ten month salaries.

Table F.

Salaries Paid for Less Than a 12-month Year in Academic Libraries							
	ALL INCUMBENTS	9-MONTH		10-MONTH*		9 AND 10 MONTH	
POSITION AND TYPE OF LIBRARY	#	#	%	#	%	#	%
Director							
Two-year college	110	3	2.7	3	2.7	6	5.5
Four-year college	104	1	<1	3	2.9	4	3.8
University	209	1	<1	3	1.4	4	1.9
Deputy/Associate/Assistant Directors							
Two-year college	52	7	13.5	3	5.8	10	19.2
Four-year college	73	2	2.7	7	9.6	9	12.3
University	361	1	<1	6	1.7	7	1.9
Department Heads/Coordinators/Senior Managers							
Two-year college	47	6	12.8	4	8.5	10	21.3
Four-year college	43	0	<1	6	14.0	6	14.0
University	315	8	2.5	11	3.5	19	6.0
Managers/Supervisors of Support Staff							
Two-year college	98	8	8.2	5	5.1	13	13.3
Four-year college	135	2	1.5	4	3.0	6	4.4
University	518	18	3.5	14	2.7	32	6.2
Librarians who do not supervise							
Two-year college	165	34	20.6	16	9.7	50	30.3
Four-year college	123	4	3.3	8	6.5	12	9.8
University	1,543	23	1.5	36	2.3	59	3.8
Beginning Librarians							
Two-year college	5	2	40.0	1	20.0	3	60.0
Four-year college	11	0	<1	0	<1	0	<1
University	108	1	<1	0	<1	1	<1

* includes 28 11-month salaries